SING A SONG OF GLADNESS

Selected Psalms FOR CHILDREN

Written by Candace Clayton
Illustrated by Don Kueker

ARCH Books

COPYRIGHT © 1974 BY CONCORDIA PUBLISHING HOUSE, ST. LOUIS, MISSOURI
CONCORDIA PUBLISHING HOUSE LTD., LONDON. E. C. 1
MANUFACTURED IN THE UNITED STATES OF AMERICA
ALL RIGHTS RESERVED
ISBN 0-570-06087-7

PSALM 8

I look at the sky, which You have made,
At the myriad lights glowing there,
And I ask, "What am I that You think of me?
Oh, Lord, what am I that You care?"

You've made me to rule this glorious world,
You've crowned me Your child and heir.
Oh, Lord, I can only sing Your praise
When I see how much You care!

PSALM 19

God's glory echoes through the skies;
It whispers with the dawn
And trumpets in the setting sun
When day is almost gone.

Although they never make a sound,
God's works His goodness tell.
From voices mute the message rings:
"Praise God, for all is well!"

PSALM 23

I can feel the love of God
Surround me as I go
Through peaceful fields, by waters still,
On high paths and on low.

The things I fear all disappear,
Each snare, each enemy.
God's love directs my every step,
Surrounds me, sets me free.

psalm 24

Open the gates! Fling them wide!
The great King will come in,
The King who has defeated
Evil, death, and sin.

His kingdom cannot falter;
He rules from shore to shore.
Open the gates! Fling them wide!
Sing praise forevermore!

psalm 37

Do not be sad because you lack
Some things that money buys.
The people knowing only gold
Know only that which dies.

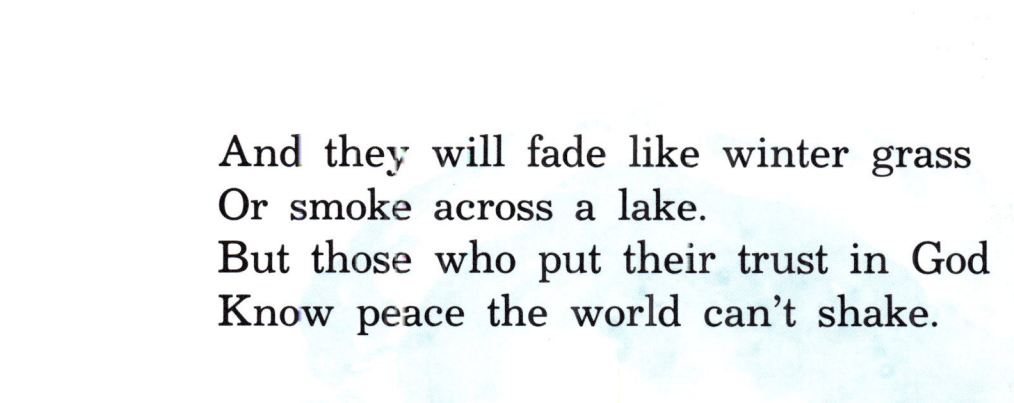

And they will fade like winter grass
Or smoke across a lake.
But those who put their trust in God
Know peace the world can't shake.

PSALM 40

I cried out to the Lord for help
And He was listening.
He took me from my pit of gloom;
He taught me how to sing.

And now I sing His song so all
Will see what God can do,
Will turn to Him when they are lost,
Will sing a new song too.

PSALM 69

Sometimes I feel completely lost,
And no one cares for me.
I have no friend to turn to,
No answer to my plea.

I walk alone in trouble;
My path seems dark and wild.
But then the God who loves me
Whispers, "You're My child."

PSALM 73

For a while I tried to understand
Why certain nasty folk
Seem to live a carefree life,
And treat pain as a joke.

They make fun, they speak evil,
They thrive on violence,
And yet they seem to prosper.
I didn't see the sense.

But God taught me the answer:
Evil isn't as it seems.
Its power grows in darkness,
But vanishes like dreams.

psalm 96

Roar, oceans, with a mighty sound;
Fields, come alive with song;
Shout your joy out loud, you woods!
Your God is great and strong.

Sing a new song to the Lord,
Creatures large and small!
People, pause and sing to Him,
For He has saved us all.

PSALM 100

Sing a song with all your heart;
Show God that you are glad
That He made snow and butterflies.
It's no time to be sad.

God made you and God made me.
We all belong to Him.
Our God is good, so sing your praise
With choirs of seraphim.

PSALM 104

You use the clouds as Your chariot,
You walk on the wind's swift wings.
The heavens You stretch out like a tent
And all creation sings.

The cedars that rustle in the breeze
House jewel-colored birds.
And in green valleys cattle graze
While mountains hide goat herds.

Countless creatures roam the land
Or swim in the ocean's roar.
You feed them from Your bounteous hand.
You give enough and more.

PSALM 108

Wake up, my soul, wake up and sing
Of what your Lord has done.
Shout praises through the morning mist
And wake the sleepy sun.

Wake up, my harp, and let His praise
Resound from every string.
His love is great and good and sure.
Wake up, oh world, and sing!

PSALM 121

I look to the mountains and call to the Lord;
My way seems so rocky and steep.
But still I am sure that the Lord hears my prayer
Our God does not slumber nor sleep.

The Lord will protect me; He'll stay by my side
In sunlight, in night's silver glow.
No danger can harm me; He'll keep me secure
In His love as I come, as I go.

psalm 146

I know there is no king on earth
As mighty, Lord, as You,
No president or queen alive
Who loves us as You do.

You set the prisoners free again,
You make the blind to see,
And, best of all, Your kingdom lasts
Through all eternity.

PSALM 147

Grass grows green upon the hill
And drinks the gentle rain.
The countless stars are scattered wide
And each one has a name.

The winds blow warm across the wheat,
The rivers flow to seas,
The horse runs swift, the bird soars high.
Praise God for all of these.

DEAR PARENTS:

Prayers for forgiveness, hymns of praise, pleas for help, declarations that help is certain to come, cries from a nation, whispers from one person: these are the psalms. And they speak as truly for today's hearts as they did for those of long ago Israel. How many of us have looked at a night sky studded with stars and marveled at man's apparent insignificance and the miracle of God's love?

David and the other psalmists must have experienced deep joy in expressing their thoughts to and about God in such beautiful forms. It might not be a bad idea for more people today, including children, to try the same activity—to write out some of their own prayers and thoughts as beautifully as possible, and to incorporate into these expressions their knowledge and joy through Jesus Christ, a dimension David could only dimly foresee.

THE EDITOR